the stuff that stuff is made of

Things We Make with Plants

Jonathan Drori

MAGIC CAT 😺 PUBLISHING

What can you see right now that was made with plants? The wood for your bookshelf or your pencil, of course. The chocolate or nuts in your snack—they're obvious, too. But what about the fiber for your t-shirt, or the rubber for the car tires outside? And here's a challenge: What can you see right now that *wasn't* made using plants? A lot less than you think!

When I was about twelve years old, I remember visiting a botanic garden bursting with plants of every shape, size, and color, from minuscule mosses to towering trees. Some of them had colossal leaves or gaudy flowers; others had sharp spikes or the feel of velvet. Some smelled sweet while others were so poisonous I wasn't even allowed to touch them. Later, I discovered that plants are not just weird and wonderful, but we literally can't live without them.

Plants are very special. Imagine being a plant: having to grow up, defend yourself from critters that come to eat you, make new seeds and disperse them . . . all while rooted to the ground! I find it even more incredible that plants are made from just two main ingredients. The first is carbon dioxide, an invisible gas in the air around us, that enters through the leaves. The second is water, which comes up through the roots. The way that plants use the energy from sunshine to turn these into more complex, solid stuff has a fancy name—photosynthesis. With just a smattering of other nutrients from the soil, plants make roots, leaves, stems, flowers, fruit, bark, and seeds.

Of course, we depend on plants for our food, but I'm fascinated by the countless ways plants have evolved for their own purposes that have made them so important to us. For example, the fibers that keep a stem sturdy or help seeds to fly on the wind can be spun into thread to make our clothes. And we use wood for building, for fuel, for making musical instruments and cricket bats, and in countless other ways. Once you look, the things people have made with plants are everywhere . . . in food and clothing, perfumes and dyes, from towering scaffolding and the heatshield of the space shuttle, to popcorn, chocolate bars, and ice cream. And even the book that you're holding right now!

Some of the plants in this book have very sad histories. Just a few generations ago, extremely valuable crops—sugarcane and cotton, for example—depended on people who had been kidnapped and enslaved. Mostly from West Africa, enslaved people were transported and forced to work in terrible conditions on plantations in the Caribbean and the United States. I remember my father explaining to me how landowners, companies, and whole countries became wealthy, buying and selling people and the things they produced. It wasn't until the 19th century that slavery was abolished.

Other plant stories—peppercorns as money, dandelion clocks, or henna designs on the skin of brides-to-be—make me smile. Be amazed, as I was, by the people who bred measly wild plants into sturdy food crops. Discover ingenious uses for plants and the incredible things people have made from them. Especially, let's celebrate the plants themselves: the most intricate and beautiful chemical factories you could possibly imagine. Three cheers for each and every plant . . . **the stuff that stuff is made of!**

—Jonathan Drori

Contents

Fruits, roots, and shoots! Discover 30 amazing plants and the wonderful things we make with them.

4 · **Vanilla**
Vanilla planifolia

6 · **Tea**
Camellia sinensis

8 · **Mandrake**
Mandragora officinarum

10 · **Papyrus**
Cyperus papyrus

12 · **Cacao**
Theobroma cacao

14 · **Cork Oak**
Quercus suber

16 · **Pine**
Pinus—various species

18 · **Giant Kelp**
Macrocystis pyrifera

20 · **Rubber**
Hevea brasiliensis

22 · **Blue Gum**
Eucalyptus globulus

24 · **Cotton**
Gossypium

26 · **Giant Timber Bamboo**
Phyllostachys reticulata

28 · **Potato**
Solanum tuberosum

30 · **Gutta-Percha**
Palaquium gutta

32 · **Corn**
Zea mays

34 · **Dandelion**
Taraxacum officinale

36 · **Prickly Pear**
Opuntia ficus-indica

38 · **Sugarcane**
Saccharum officinarum

40 · **Pumpkin**
The cucurbit family

42 · **Nutmeg**
Myristica fragrans

44 · **Henna**
Lawsonia inermis

46 · **Rice**
Oryza sativa

48 · **Black Pepper**
Piper nigrum

50 · **Beech**
Fagus sylvatica

52 · **Olive**
Olea europaea

54 · **Wheat**
Triticum aestivum

56 · **Baobab**
Adansonia digitata

58 · **Tomato**
Solanum lycopersicum

60 · **Coconut**
Cocos nucifera

62 · **Peanut**
Arachis hypogaea

Vanilla. Sometimes belittled as boring or plain, vanilla is anything but! True vanilla is one of the most valuable and delicious spices in the world.

PROBABLY A THOUSAND YEARS AGO, the indigenous Totonac people of Mexico began to cultivate the vanilla orchid, meaning that they grew and harvested it.

THEY BELIEVED VANILLA WAS A SACRED GIFT from the Gods that came from the blood of a mythical princess.

IT WAS SO VALUABLE that the invading Aztecs forced the Totonacs to pay taxes with vanilla pods (and cocoa beans!). In the 1520s, Spanish conquerors brought vanilla pods from Mexico back to Spain. They were an immediate hit for flavoring chocolate.

IN THE LATE 1700S, THE FRENCH TRIED TO GROW VANILLA on the islands of Réunion and Mauritius in the Indian Ocean. The plants grew well and had plenty of flowers, but they never produced any pods. That's because these islands weren't home to the special kinds of birds and bees that flit between the flowers to fertilize them.

IN 1841 EDMOND ALBIUS, an enslaved boy working on a farm on Réunion, found a way to do this job of fertilization himself. Using a little sliver of bamboo, he cut the membrane between the male and female parts of the vanilla flower and squeezed them together for a few seconds. Two to three weeks later, a pod grew—thanks to his helping hand!

MOST VANILLA NOW COMES FROM BIG PLANTATIONS in Madagascar and Indonesia, but every single vanilla pod is the result of this technique invented nearly two hundred years ago by twelve-year-old Edmond.

VANILLA FLOWERS OPEN ONLY FOR A SINGLE DAY, so farmers must employ people to search every morning for the ones that are open and ready to pollinate. This means that vanilla is still very expensive, so much so that most vanilla flavoring doesn't come from the vanilla orchid at all but instead contains a substance called vanillin, which is made in factories from chipped wood. Natural vanilla extract contains vanillin, too, but about two hundred other flavorful chemicals as well, which means it smells and tastes much more interesting.

If you have a chance to taste ice cream or hot chocolate made with natural vanilla, or sniff a jar of sugar in which a vanilla pod has been kept, you will discover why it has been prized for centuries.

Tea. The emerald-green leaves of the tea plant are used to make one of the world's most popular drinks.

WHILE THE NATURAL CAFFEINE IN TEA helps the plant to defend itself against pests, and even discourages other plants from growing nearby, it makes a refreshing and stimulating drink for us! People first began drinking tea in China about 2,000 years ago, and the Portuguese brought it to Europe in the 16th century. It became especially fashionable in England but remained an expensive luxury until the 19th century, when Britain set up large tea plantations in India and tea became a drink that most people could afford.

THE TEA TRADE WAS BIG BUSINESS. In the mid-19th century, American and British sailors competed to bring back the freshest cargoes of tea in sleek, ultrafast ships known as clippers.

TO MAKE GREEN TEA, FRESH TEA LEAVES ARE HEATED, pressed, and dried, which takes away much of the mouth-puckering bitter taste and leaves a seaweedy, grassy, or toasty flavor.

TO MAKE A CUP OF TEA, the dried green or black tea leaves are steeped in hot water to release the flavors. In China and Japan, the everyday drink is green tea.

TEA IS SERVED IN MANY WAYS AROUND THE WORLD. In India, tea leaves are simmered in milk and water, with sugar, cinnamon, cloves, and cardamom. In the Himalayas, black tea is mixed with yak butter and salt. Some Europeans drink tea with a slice of lemon, while in North America it's often iced. In Russia, hot black tea is sometimes served with a lump of sugar or a small dish of jam on the side. Many British drinkers prefer their tea with a splash of milk and a spoonful of sugar, along with a biscuit to dunk in the hot liquid. Perhaps the most peculiar is boba tea, which contains milk, added flavorings and chewy balls of tapioca, drunk through an especially large 'boba straw'.

BLACK TEA is made by leaving the plucked leaves to wilt before being squashed between rollers and allowed to ferment for several hours. This releases exciting floral and fruity flavors.

During Chinese wedding celebrations the bride and groom serve tea to their future families.

Tea

Camellia sinensis

Originally from Southeast Asia, tea is now grown around the world in warm or hot climates with plenty of light and rainfall.

Tea is often cultivated on hills where the plants grow more slowly, giving the **LEAVES** a better flavor.

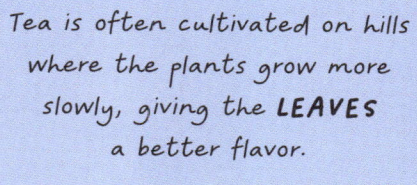

Left to itself, tea grows as an evergreen shrub or a small tree, but for ease of picking, it is usually sown in rows in large plantations and pruned to chest height.

If tea is allowed to flower, its white or cream **BLOSSOMS** are followed by small greenish-brown **FRUIT** containing a few round seeds.

The best tea comes from young **BUDS** and **LEAVES**, which are hand-plucked every two weeks during the growing season.

Young leaves, which are tender and vulnerable, also contain the most **CAFFEINE**, a natural pesticide.

Straight from the bush, tea leaves taste horribly bitter, which discourages animals from eating them. The pleasant flavor of tea depends on proper preparation of the leaves to make either green tea or black tea.

Mandrake. At Hogwarts, the school for wizards in the Harry Potter stories, mandrake plants have strangely human qualities and are cultivated for their magical powers. In real life, the mandrake is certainly powerful, and even associated with witchcraft.

BEFORE THE ARTIFICIAL ANESTHETICS OF THE MID-19TH CENTURY, all painkilling drugs came from plants, of which mandrake was one of the most important. Ancient Greek surgeons gave their patients an anesthetic of mandrake root mixed with wine, while Ancient Roman patients were given a piece of root to chew on before an operation.

MANDRAKE NUMBS THE BODY BUT ALSO CAUSES HALLUCINATIONS—visions of things that aren't really there. In higher doses, it can temporarily make a person appear to be dead, and it can even kill. At a time of little scientific knowledge, the doll-like mandrake root's powers seemed supernatural.

IN MEDIEVAL EUROPE, THOSE WHO KNEW MOST ABOUT THE MYSTERIES OF MANDRAKES AND OTHER PLANTS WERE HEALERS AND HERBALISTS—often older women. Their detailed knowledge of what many people thought was evil magic meant they risked being accused of witchcraft. Curiously, one of the chemicals in mandrake gives the sensation of flight—the likely origin of the belief in witches flying on broomsticks.

MANDRAKE ROOTS WERE SOLD AS AMULETS—charms to ward off bad spirits. Sometimes, mandrake-sellers would pierce tiny holes in the "head" of a root, filling them with grass seeds. When they sprouted, the "hairy little man" looked even more convincing and could be sold for a higher price.

MANDRAKES WERE SO VALUABLE THAT HEALERS OR TRADERS DELIBERATELY SPREAD SPINE-CHILLING RUMORS to discourage others from picking them. From Roman times to the 17th century, a common belief was that when a mandrake was uprooted, its intense shrieks could kill. The obvious solution was to plug your ears with beeswax, tie the plant to a dog, and throw a chunk of meat so that by chasing it, the dog could safely yank the root from the ground.

Today, there are perfumes and cosmetics named *mandrake* and *mandragora*, which even now conjure up a mood of excitement and mischief.

Mandrake
Mandragora officinarum

A stemless, straggly little plant from the Mediterranean, mandrake enjoys full sun at the edges of fields and in olive groves.

Clusters of **FLOWERS** vary in color from greenish-white to dusky purple. Each bloom is the shape of an upturned bell.

Mandrake **FRUIT** change color as they ripen, from glossy pea-green to an inviting gold, although their earthy scent is peculiar.

A mandrake's **ROOT**, which grows to be about one foot long, sometimes forks in two here and there. With a little imagination, it can resemble a miniature person, complete with head, arms, and legs.

The plant belongs to the same family as tomatoes and its fruit look temptingly similar, but beware: the mandrake is **DEADLY**! All parts should be avoided, but especially the roots, which contain powerful poisons to ward off foraging insects and animals.

Dark lettuce-like **LEAVES** grow from the center, no more than ankle height.

Papyrus. Beautiful, towering papyrus was a versatile treasure of the ancient world.

PAPYRUS CLUMPS PROVIDE SHELTER FOR ANIMALS AND SLOW THE FLOW OF WATER, trapping nutrient-rich silt. For ancient Egyptians, the papyrus swamps of the Nile River delta were a living larder, full of fresh fish and game birds. They also cooked and ate the pith of papyrus stems, carved its woody underground parts for tools, and burned it as fuel. Women used their teeth to strip the tough outer layer of the stems to make string for baskets, nets, and mats.

EVEN THE ROPE USED TO SHIFT HUGE STONES FOR THE PYRAMIDS WAS MADE FROM PAPYRUS. It was such an important plant to the ancient Egyptians that they carved papyrus designs into many of their palaces, temples, and tombs.

AROUND 3000 BC, ANCIENT EGYPTIANS INVENTED A PAPERLIKE WRITING MATERIAL MADE FROM PAPYRUS. To make it, layers of pith from the stems were laid crisscrossed on top of each other, then soaked and pounded together before being pressed flat, dried, and "polished" with powdered clay. Papyrus sheets or scrolls were the main writing materials in ancient Greece and Rome and were used in Egypt right up until 900 AD.

PAPYRUS SWAMPS ARE UNCOMMON IN EGYPT NOW because the land has been reclaimed for growing crops, but they cover huge areas of Central and East Africa. In the Sudd of South Sudan, one of the world's largest wetlands where they are a source of food and a home for wildlife, sheaves of papyrus stems are still bundled together to make boats—just as in ancient Egypt, thousands of years ago.

The word *papyrus*, from ancient Greek, is the origin of the modern word for paper in many languages. And papyrus pith, from which the earliest paper was made, was *biblos*, which gives us words such as *Bible*.

Papyrus
Cyperus papyrus

Papyrus inhabits steamy swamps and shallow riverbanks, growing in dense clumps of stems as thick as your wrist and often 16 feet tall.

The soaring **STEMS** sway in the slightest breeze, but thick vegetation and sluggish water make papyrus swamps unexpectedly quiet places. Shhhhh!

A starburst of slim **BRANCHES** sits atop each stem, with a spike of little greenish-brown flowers at the tip of each branch.

Although papyrus resembles bamboo, it is not a grass, but a **SEDGE**. Unlike grasses, sedges don't have any joints in their smooth, straight stems, which are triangular rather than circular.

Each stem has a tough, stringy outer **SKIN**. This surrounds a soft white **PITH**, which contains air pockets protected by strong bundles of fibers. These hollow sections enable papyrus to float well—great for making boats!

Cacao. *Theobroma*, the scientific name for the cacao tree, means "food of the Gods", while *cacao* is the name of the tree and the unprocessed beans.

THE FIRST CHOCOLATE BARS WERE MADE IN ENGLAND in 1847—before then chocolate had always been a drink. Ancient people in South America 5,000 years ago made a bitter beverage from cacao beans, and the ancient Olmec and Maya civilizations of Mexico and Central America even had cacao orchards. By the 15th century, the Aztecs were making hot chocolate by whisking unsweetened ground cacao beans with boiling water, vanilla, a kick of chili pepper and cornmeal to thicken it.

THE AZTECS CALLED THIS DRINK XOCOATL (SHO-KWA-TIL), which is where our word *chocolate* comes from. It was a drink for the elite and a boost for soldiers. Bloodred coloring was added for religious ceremonies. As well as being nutritious, cacao contains theobromine, a gentle pick-me-up. Stimulating and sacred, cacao beans were very valuable, and the Aztecs even used them as currency.

WHEN THE SPANISH BROUGHT CACAO BEANS TO EUROPE in the 1500s, they changed the drink's recipe, adding sugar and milk and leaving out the chili and coloring. By the 17th century it was all the rage and served in special cafés known as chocolate houses.

WHEN CACAO PODS ARE PICKED AND SPLIT OPEN, natural bacteria and yeasts get to work, developing a chocolatey flavor. After a week, the beans are sun-dried and roasted. The cacao inside is ground smooth to create chocolate liquor—a thick, oily paste that can be used for baking just as it is. The liquor can also be separated into cocoa butter, a fat used to make white chocolate, and dark brown cocoa, which is powdered for drinks and ice cream. Mmmm . . .

TO MAKE A CHOCOLATE BAR, warm cocoa is combined with ingredients such as sugar, milk powder, and vanilla, and cocoa butter is added for melt-in-your-mouth smoothness. After careful stirring, the mixture is poured into molds to cool and set. Some fancy bars are made by hand.

Today, homemade hot chocolate, made with plenty of real cocoa and a dash of vanilla, is the best thing ever.

Cacao
Theobroma cacao

Cacao originated in South American rainforests, although most now comes from West Africa, where it is planted in the shade of other trees.

Cacao's dainty, thimble-sized **FLOWERS** seem out of place, growing straight from the tree's trunk and large branches. They are pollinated by tiny, biting midges.

The **FRUIT** takes about six months to ripen into leathery pods, each the size of a junior football and attached to the tree by stubby stalks.

The **PODS** can be yellow, orange, or even deep purple. Depending on the variety, each one contains around thirty to fifty large pink seeds, or beans.

Cacao is dispersed by animals that are attracted to the sweet, wholesome mush that surrounds its beans. Monkeys can gulp the **BEANS** whole, later dropping them in their poo. Smaller animals, such as rodents and bats, spread cacao when they eat the mush and spit and scatter the bitter beans.

Cork Oak. Cork is one of the world's super-materials, with many surprising uses.

CORK IS MOST COMMONLY USED TO MAKE THE STOPPERS IN WINE BOTTLES. It's perfectly safe and neither liquids nor air can get through it, so the wine won't spoil. Cork can be cut and squeezed into the neck of a bottle, where it will stay firmly in position—the stopper even makes a pleasing *pop* when it's pulled out! About 13 billion cork wine stoppers, or corks, are made every year, mostly by machines that stamp them from thick strips of cork bark using powerful hole punches.

CORK CAN BE A TREAT FOR THE FEET. Roman women wore cork-soled sandals, which were very light, durable, and didn't get soggy in puddles. Two thousand years later, cork is still used this way. And because heat does not flow well through cork, it's ideal for bathroom floors. Cork tiles feel warm underfoot because they insulate—the heat from your feet stays in your feet!

CORK IS FULL OF MINUSCULE POCKETS OF TRAPPED AIR, WHICH MAKE IT VERY GOOD AT ABSORBING SOUND WAVES. Places that mustn't sound harsh or echoey, such as concert halls and recording studios, sometimes use cork panels on their walls for soundproofing.

SURPRISINGLY FOR SUCH A TRADITIONAL MATERIAL, CORK IS OFTEN FOUND IN NASA'S MOST ADVANCED SPACECRAFT. Lightweight, fireproof, and an excellent insulator, it is used in the cladding of launch rockets and fuel tanks, and in the shields of nosecones, to protect them from the extreme heat of reentry into the atmosphere. Cork gives protection from floating space debris, too!

CORK FORESTS ARE VERY IMPORTANT ECOSYSTEMS. The many plants that grow there provide a home for species that would otherwise be threatened, like the Iberian lynx and Spanish imperial eagle. Domesticated turkeys, sheep, and snuffling pigs forage for acorns, and in turn produce meat, cheese, and wool for humans. The ecosystem supports more than 100,000 people in southern Europe and North Africa.

The more cork we use, the more we support the trees, plants, and animals that live in cork forests and the people who depend on them. Hooray for cork!

Cork Oak
Quercus suber

Cork oaks are slow-growing and long-lived trees with low, twisted branches and a large evergreen canopy.

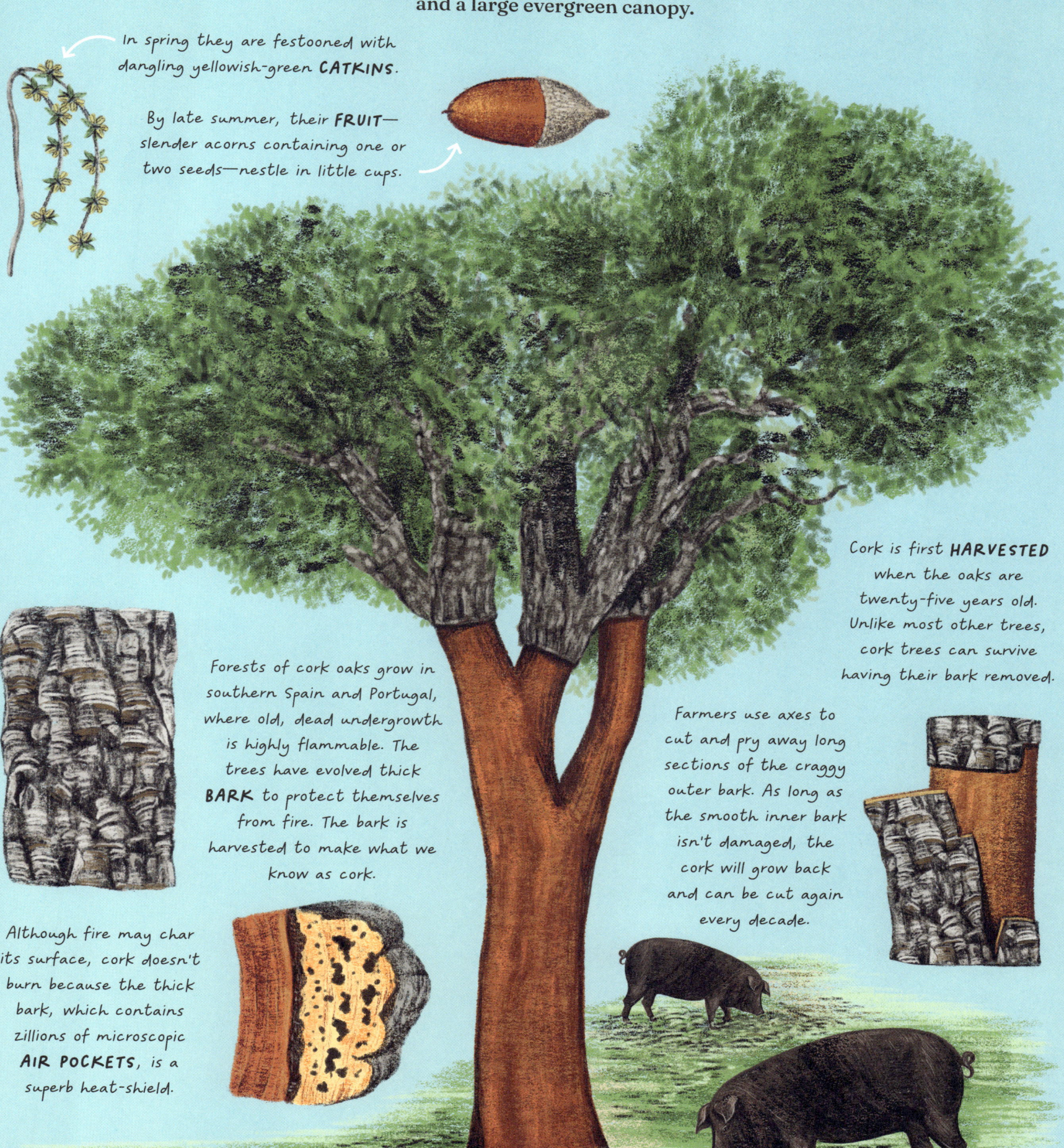

In spring they are festooned with dangling yellowish-green **CATKINS**.

By late summer, their **FRUIT**—slender acorns containing one or two seeds—nestle in little cups.

Forests of cork oaks grow in southern Spain and Portugal, where old, dead undergrowth is highly flammable. The trees have evolved thick **BARK** to protect themselves from fire. The bark is harvested to make what we know as cork.

Although fire may char its surface, cork doesn't burn because the thick bark, which contains zillions of microscopic **AIR POCKETS**, is a superb heat-shield.

Cork is first **HARVESTED** when the oaks are twenty-five years old. Unlike most other trees, cork trees can survive having their bark removed.

Farmers use axes to cut and pry away long sections of the craggy outer bark. As long as the smooth inner bark isn't damaged, the cork will grow back and can be cut again every decade.

Pine. In the Age of Sail, when huge wooden ships were roaming the seven seas, pine was in great demand.

THE IMPRESSIVELY TALL AND STRAIGHT TRUNKS OF SOME SPECIES OF PINE WERE USED TO MAKE SHIPS' MASTS, while wads of hemp or cotton soaked in pine tar were wedged between the timbers of a ship's hull to make it watertight.

PINE IS ALSO USED TO MAKE PAPER. While the ancient Egyptians made a paper-like material with papyrus (page 10), about 2,000 years ago Chinese paper makers started making the kind of paper we recognize today. They ground up plants and mulberry bark in water and poured the mixture through a flat sieve. The water drained away, leaving a thin mat of fibers that were dried in the sun.

TODAY, MOST PAPER IS MADE USING THE SAME PRINCIPLE BUT FROM WOOD, ESPECIALLY FROM PINE AND SPRUCE TREES, and by colossal machines, some as wide as a football field and several times as long! Pines are harvested when they're about six to eight years old and then pulped with mechanical grinders and water, or using a chemical soup. The resulting slurry is sprayed onto a continuously moving fine wire mesh, leaving a thin, wet mat of millions of tiny higgledy-piggledy fibers.

CHEMICALS SUCH AS STARCH ARE ADDED TO MAKE THE PAPER FEEL SMOOTHER, or minerals like clay to add body. Finally, the pulpy mat is squeezed between gigantic rollers so the fibers intertwine to form a solid, smooth, continuous sheet, which is dried and wound onto colossal rolls that can be more than 13 feet high, 32 feet wide, and weigh 60 tons each! The rolls are delivered to factories, where they are cut to different sizes. One tree yields about 10,000 sheets of paper!

PINEWOOD IS ALSO USED FOR BUILDING HOMES AND ROOFS and for making furniture, doors and window frames. The tree's seeds, or pine nuts, can be eaten just as they are, or blitzed with basil and Parmesan cheese to make pesto sauce for pasta. At Christmas, fragrant young pines are festooned with colored lights and ornaments.

In Korea, *sollipcha* is a traditional tea made with pine needles, pine pollen, and a dash of honey.

Pine

Pinus—various species

There are more than one hundred species of pine trees, spread all over the world.

Although most pine trees are native to cooler northern countries and mountainous areas, some species grow in Mediterranean climates and even on sand dunes.

Pines keep their needles all year round, which allows the trees to make food even in winter.

Their leaves, or **NEEDLES,** are narrow and waxy, preventing them from losing water in freezing, dry air.

Pine trees are conifers—plants that bear **CONES** rather than flowers or fruit. Pollen from male cones is carried on the wind.

Female cones develop seeds and drop to the ground to germinate.

Growing superbly straight, most pine **BRANCHES** slope upward but have the flexibility to bend downward under the weight of snow.

If a tree is injured or attacked by insects, it can self-seal its wounds using antiseptic **RESIN,** protecting itself from further infection. We associate pine's fresh scent with hygiene—it's often added to soaps and household cleaners.

In some species, the cones produce nutlike **SEEDS** that can be eaten and dispersed by birds (or eaten by us!).

Giant Kelp. There are more than 12,000 different species of seaweed, from delicate pink and blue-green varieties that flutter like watery handkerchiefs near the seashore, to the vast, brown giant kelp of deeper waters.

FORESTS OF GIANT KELP TEEM WITH LIFE. They are hatcheries and nurseries for young fish, and gardens for limpets, crabs, and sea urchins. They are also an abundant hunting ground for seals. The many creatures they support may have fed the first people who journeyed to North America around the northern rim of the Pacific Ocean about 15,000 years ago.

MOST SEAWEEDS ARE EDIBLE AND ARE AN ESPECIALLY POPULAR FOOD IN EAST ASIA, where various useful ingredients are extracted from them to add to other foods. For example, in Japan, kombu, a variety of kelp, was the original source of the flavor enhancer monosodium glutamate (MSG).

THE MOST IMPORTANT SUBSTANCES WE EXTRACT FROM GIANT KELP AND OTHER BROWN SEAWEEDS ARE ALGINATES. These chemicals have hundreds of uses, mostly related to their ability to hold on to water and form jellylike materials. In foods, alginates act as stabilizers and thickeners. They make ice cream smooth and prevent pesky ice crystals from forming. They're used to thicken sauces, syrups, and chocolate milk. They make bread and cakes fluffier, cream cheese taste creamier, and in just tiny amounts, they make the head on beer foamier.

ALGINATES ARE USED IN MEDICINE AND INDUSTRY, TOO. They're used in bandages and wound dressings and are added to medicinal tablets to help them break down in the stomach. They thicken house paints so they don't drip, and they are used in products that must hold water and in which the ingredients must not separate, such as toothpaste, lipstick, face masks, and hand lotions.

IN CALIFORNIA, DURING THE FIRST WORLD WAR, giant kelp was fermented in huge vats to make acetone, an ingredient used in explosives. People who lived near acetone factories complained bitterly about the awfully smelly process.

Giant kelp is sustainably harvested by cutting off just the top few feet several times a year. Commercial harvesters use large ships with machines that look like giant hedge trimmers.

Giant Kelp
Macrocystis pyrifera

Seaweeds are algae—simple organisms that lack many of the internal structures of land plants.

Seaweeds thrive in cool water. They are found all over the world, and giant kelp, which is the **WORLD'S LARGEST SEAWEED**, grows near the shore, where it forms huge underground forests.

It can grow up to 164 feet long, and quickly too, adding 20 inches a day or more if conditions are right. That's as fast as the fastest-growing bamboo!

Hollow air-filled **BLADDERS** ensure the fronds float upward toward the light.

The **STIPE** is a simple, sturdy stem that supports kelp's flat fronds—smooth, leathery ribbons also known as **BLADES**.

Kelp's **HOLDFAST** may look like a root, but it doesn't draw up nutrients or water. Instead, it anchors the seaweed to the ocean floor, so it doesn't float away.

Kelp plants may grow for up to ten years, but individual **FRONDS** live just a few months.

Rubber. Long before European explorers arrived in South America, the indigenous people of Brazil and Venezuela used rubber latex to make shoes, containers, and bottles.

IN LONDON IN THE LATE 18TH CENTURY, LITTLE CUBES OF RUBBER were sold as erasers for rubbing out pencil marks, which is how rubber got its English name.

IN THE 1920S, THE SCOTTISH CHEMIST CHARLES MACINTOSH used a latex mixture to make waterproof raincoats. Early versions were alarmingly heavy and very sweaty!

IN 1839, THE AMERICAN INVENTOR CHARLES GOODYEAR heated rubber and sulfur and found that the result, later called vulcanized rubber, was extraordinarily tough. Rubber became a new wonder material, and was used to make everything from shoes and sneakers to bellows for pumping air into furnaces and even false teeth! We now know that more than 2,500 years before Goodyear's discovery, the Olmec people of South America made large, heavy rubber balls for a team sport they played in long, narrow courts where they bounced the balls off the side walls.

RUBBER BECAME SO VALUABLE that in the late 19th century, the British took rubber seeds from Brazil to develop huge plantations in their colonies in South and Southeast Asia. Today, this region is still the source of most of the world's rubber.

IN 1888, ANOTHER SCOT, CHARLES DUNLOP, INVENTED THE INFLATABLE RUBBER BICYCLE TIRE, and by the early 20th century, the motor industry depended on rubber for tires, engine parts, and windshield wipers. In 1928, Henry Ford, who founded the Ford Motor Company, objected to British control of the world's rubber supply and set up his own plantation and factory in a huge clearing in the Amazon rainforest. The trees, which had been planted too close together, sadly succumbed to disease.

TODAY, RUBBER IS EVERYWHERE, from flooring, firehoses, boots, and huge truck tires to cleaning gloves, super-stretchy rubber bands, and festive party balloons.

A typical tree produces 17-22 pounds of rubber per year—enough for several car tires, or tens of thousands of rubber bands!

Rubber
Hevea brasiliensis

Deep in the wilds of the Amazon rainforest, rubber trees compete for light, soaring more than 130 feet tall. Cultivated trees are much smaller.

Rainforest trees of the same species are often separated from each other by many other plants jostling for space in the thick vegetation.

Rubber trees defend themselves with a creamy latex, a mixture of rubber and water that oozes from special vessels in the **BARK** when it is damaged. The sticky latex is difficult for insects to wade through and it sets to form a germproof coating.

So, to help insects that are flitting between open flowers that may be far apart, rubber trees **BLOSSOM** at the same time, by responding to tiny changes in sunlight.

Rubber trees produce small, inedible, yellow-green **FRUITS**. Once ripe, they explode with a loud bang, each one flinging out three large, mottled **SEEDS** that can float on floodwater to sprout elsewhere.

If a spiral groove is carved into the rubber tree's bark, the **LATEX** that flows downward along the cut can be collected in a cup. On rubber plantations, trees are tapped for their latex every two or three days. The latex is sieved, refined, washed, and dried, leaving a rubbery material.

Blue Gum. Gum trees are brimming with strongly scented substances.

THE BLUE MOUNTAINS OF SOUTHEASTERN AUSTRALIA, where many species of eucalyptus, such as blue gum, evolved, take their name from the haze in the air caused by oils and resins evaporating from the trees' leaves.

EUCALYPTUS OIL IS EXTRACTED FROM THE LEAVES AND STEMS using steam and has a fresh, minty scent. It's added to cough drops and cold remedies, mouthwash and disinfectant. The timber contains a sticky resin, or sap, which resists rot, making it an excellent material for construction, fencing, and furniture. It's also pulped to make paper and heated to make charcoal.

IN THEIR NATIVE ENVIRONMENT, EUCALYPTUS TREES SUPPORT PLENTY OF WILDLIFE, including koalas, possums, and many birds and beetles. However, when eucalyptus is planted abroad, where animals and insects haven't evolved to digest the plant, it can become invasive—meaning that it sometimes spreads out of control.

EUCALYPTUS OIL IS HIGHLY FLAMMABLE, so the trees have had to adapt to ferocious bushfires. The seeds, snug in their woody capsules, often survive the extreme heat. And some species produce 'lignotubers'—huge swollen underground roots that weigh up to 1,100 pounds each (as much as a grand piano!). These store enough food to enable trees to sprout again, even after fire has destroyed everything above ground.

DIDGERIDOOS ARE AN INDIGENOUS AUSTRALIAN WIND INSTRUMENT, traditionally made from three-to-six-foot lengths of eucalyptus trunks or branches that have been attacked by termites. The insects nibble away the dead heartwood at the center but avoid the living outer layers, which are protected by resin, leaving behind a hollow tube full of air traps and tunnels. These create a deep, throbbing, whooshing sound when air is blown into the instrument.

WITH THEIR DEEP ROOTS, some eucalyptus trees are able to draw up microscopic particles of gold, which become concentrated in their leaves. There's not enough to be valuable, but it can be detected using special instruments and may provide a handy clue to the location of worthwhile gold deposits deep underground.

Eucalyptus trees have a cunning trick to prevent competition—they make and release chemicals that discourage other plant species from growing nearby.

Blue Gum
Eucalyptus globulus

There are hundreds of eucalyptus species, almost all of them evergreen and native to Australia.

Eucalyptus trees are also known as gum trees because of the sticky **RESIN** that seeps from their trunks and branches.

Eucalyptus globulus, or the **BLUE GUM**, is the most commonly planted eucalyptus species. Fast-growing and sturdy, it is grown worldwide in large plantations and can be harvested after just five to seven years.

Some eucalyptus species have extraordinarily beautiful **BARK**. The blue-gray bark peels off in ribbons to reveal patches of bright green, which change to blue, purple, and brick red with exposure to the air.

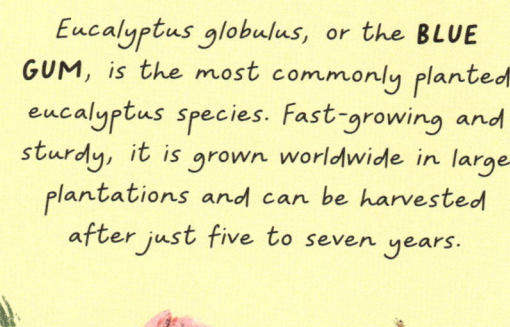

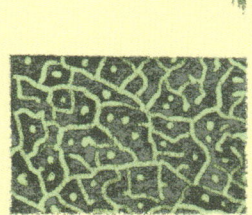

Thousands of tiny **OIL GLANDS** in the eucalyptus leaf make pungent chemicals to ward off insects, bacteria, and fungi.

Eucalyptus **FRUITS**, known as gumnuts, are hard, woody capsules containing many small seeds. They're important food for birds such as galahs, cockatoos, and parrots.

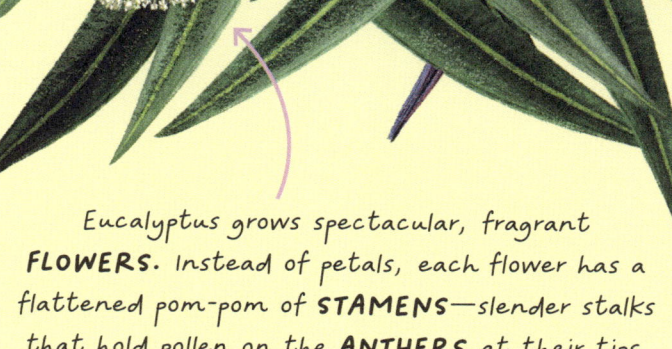

Eucalyptus grows spectacular, fragrant **FLOWERS**. Instead of petals, each flower has a flattened pom-pom of **STAMENS**—slender stalks that hold pollen on the **ANTHERS** at their tips.

Cotton. Soft and comfortable, especially in hot weather, cotton clothing was made thousands of years ago in South Asia and Central America.

INCA WARRIORS wore armor woven from thick cotton canvas. Today, cotton clothing is everywhere and cotton is the most common natural fiber in the world. It is grown in the tropics, especially India, China, and the Cotton Belt of the Southern United States.

WHEN EUROPEANS FIRST LAID THEIR HANDS ON COTTON cloth from India, brought by Arab traders, it felt to them like sheep's wool. So, when a 14th-century English travel book claimed that cotton came from a special tree that grew tiny lambs on the ends of its branches, many people believed it. The branches reportedly bent to allow the lambs to reach grass when they were hungry!

THE FIRST STEP TO MAKING COTTON THREAD IS GINNING— separating the fiber from the seeds. By hand, this is slow and painstaking work, but in 1793, American Eli Whitney of Connecticut invented a mechanical gin, a machine that enabled cotton to be mass-produced.

HUGE COTTON FACTORIES, ESPECIALLY IN ENGLAND, made thread, fabric, and finished clothes, which were sold all over the world. It was a very profitable business, but it was built on slave labor. In the first half of the 19th century, cotton was grown, picked, and prepared in the Southern United States by millions of enslaved people who had originally been captured and transported from West Africa, or who were born into slavery.

TODAY, THE HARD WORK OF PICKING THE COTTON BOLLS, separating fiber from seeds, and spinning thread is mostly done by machines. The fibers naturally have a slight twist so they cling together and can be spun into a continuous, strong, and slightly springy thread, which can be dyed and woven into textiles to make clothes. Meanwhile, the seeds are pressed to make cottonseed oil for cooking, leaving behind seedcake—a nutritious food for dairy cows.

SURPRISINGLY, COTTON FIBER IS USED TO MAKE UNITED STATES DOLLAR BILLS. The flexible, light, and durable paper is a blend of 75 percent cotton and 25 percent linen.

They say money doesn't grow on trees—but it can grow in fields!

Cotton
Gossypium

Cotton is grown as a shrubby chest-high plant—although left to itself it would become a small tree.

The **PETALS** of its pale, floppy flowers turn reddish after a day or two of blooming and eventually drop off.

The **FRUIT**—pale-green capsules, or bolls, each contain about thirty fingernail-sized seeds covered in more than 10,000 hollow white fibers.

The pressure from the **SEEDS** and **FIBERS** causes the capsules to split open, revealing soft, dazzling white bundles.

The white **FIBERS** burst out, each one thinner than a human hair and about as long as your pinkie finger.

The purpose of the **FIBERS** is to protect the seeds and help them fly on the breeze—except on farms, of course, where the bolls are picked long before the seeds and their precious fibers have a chance to float away.

Bamboo. Bamboo is a remarkable material and the plant itself is full of surprises.

MORE THAN A THOUSAND DIFFERENT SPECIES OF BAMBOO GROW WORLDWIDE, especially across South and East Asia and in places that aren't too dry or cold. Bamboo is a grass from the same family as sugarcane, wheat, and corn, which humans eat. But who dines on bamboo? Pandas! In fact, it's almost the only thing they eat.

MOST BEARS ARE OMNIVORES. Pandas are herbivores, but they have the gut of a carnivore. Therefore, they don't digest bamboo easily, so they have to spend half their lives eating and can poo up to forty times a day!

BAMBOO'S HUGE, HOLLOW STEMS hardly thicken as they age. They are as wide at the top as at the bottom.

THERE IS A SAYING IN NORTHEASTERN INDIA: "WHEN BAMBOO FLOWERS, FAMINE FOLLOWS." This is because although plenty of the seeds sprout, the huge number of them produced in a mass flowering eventually leads to an explosion in the rat population. The rats feed on the seeds, then move on to farmers' crops, causing famine and spreading disease.

BAMBOO IS BOTH STIFF AND LIGHT, MAKING IT VERY USEFUL. It's used for chopsticks, fishing rods, and as garden supports for other plants.

Bamboo's natural hollow structure makes it perfect for panpipes, flutes, and mouth organs, while the soft fibers from some species are used to make paper, fabric, and even toilet paper!

PEOPLE DON'T EAT BAMBOO SEEDS, but the young shoots are edible once they've been peeled and boiled to destroy the poisons that defend the plant from animals. These shoots are crisp and sweet—although it might seem odd eating something that might later be used to make buildings or furniture!

Bamboo stems are so strong that they can be tied together to make scaffolding for construction work on tall buildings.

Giant Timber Bamboo
Phyllostachys reticulata

Giant bamboo, originally from China, is jaw-droppingly huge.

Unlike most other plants that flower annually, most woody bamboo species flower only once and then die. Some species wait as long as one hundred years before flowering!

Remarkably, bamboos of the same kind growing in the same area produce their **FLOWERS** and **SEEDS** in unison.

There's a clever reason: Some animals really love bamboo seeds. The more they eat, the more their population grows. By making loads of seeds, but only rarely, bamboo ensures that there won't be enough animals to eat all of them. That way, more of the seeds can survive and grow.

Bamboo's vivid green **STEMS** turn golden as they age and can grow up to 82 feet.

With enough water and light, bamboo can grow three feet in a single day, making it the fastest-growing land plant on Earth. A microphone placed on a stem can pick up the sound of it growing!

Bamboo stems are like the common grasses of farms and roadsides, only much, much bigger. Like our bones, they are **HOLLOW** tubes—structures that are extremely strong for their weight.

Potato. Boiled and buttered, roasted, fried as chips or french fries, or mashed to a smooth cream . . . is there anyone who doesn't love potatoes?

WILD POTATOES ORIGINATED IN THE MOUNTAIN PLAINS between what is now Peru and northwestern Bolivia in South America.

PEOPLE STARTED GROWING THEM THERE AROUND 7,000-10,000 YEARS AGO AND TODAY THERE ARE THOUSANDS OF DIFFERENT VARIETIES with interesting flavors, shapes, and textures, and insides that can be white, yellow, orange, red, blue, or even violet.

IT'S HARD TO BELIEVE THAT POTATOES WEREN'T ALWAYS POPULAR. They were brought from South America to Europe by the Spanish in the mid-16th century, but they were slow to catch on. The potato was unfamiliar to Europeans, and people were suspicious of the nightshade family to which potatoes belong, because it includes many poisonous plants. However, rulers could see the value of a tasty and nutritious food crop that was easily grown, so they set about persuading their people that potatoes were the bee's knees.

IN THE 1740S, KING FREDERICK THE GREAT OF PRUSSIA HELD PUBLIC BANQUETS to prove that potatoes were safe and enjoyable to eat, even for royalty.

RUMORS OF ARMED GUARDS being stationed around potato fields encouraged peasant farmers to think of potatoes as so valuable that they would plant some themselves.

EVENTUALLY, POTATOES ENABLED FARMERS TO PRODUCE MORE FOOD, MORE QUICKLY, AND ON LESS LAND THAN BY GROWING GRAINS ALONE. More food meant that families could feed more children, and the boost to the population meant more people could work in factories, and so countries became wealthier.

High up in the Andes mountains, indigenous people preserve potatoes by repeatedly leaving them to freeze overnight and dry in the sun the next day. Freeze-dried potato, or chuño, can keep for years.

Potato
Solanum tuberosum

The bushy, knee-high potato plant has hairy stems and pretty, pinkish, horn-shaped flowers.

Potatoes store nutrients in their swollen underground **STEMS**, known as **TUBERS**. These allow the plant to survive the winter and sprout new plants in the spring.

Potato plants have **FRUIT**, too, although we don't often see them. They are green or dull-purplish; look like small, unripe tomatoes; and are quite poisonous. Indeed, the only parts of the potato plant that aren't toxic are the **TUBERS**.

The potatoes we eat are, in fact, these tasty tubers, filled with energy-giving goodness.

Don't eat potatoes if they're green! Green coloration, although not harmful itself, means that the potato has been exposed to light and that it is busy making **POISONS** to stop animals from eating it.

To grow more potato plants, the tubers themselves are cut into pieces and planted. New **STEMS** grow from the tuber's eyes—little pits on the tuber's skin that contain tiny buds.

29 | Potato

Gutta-Percha. The gutta-percha tree produces latex—a sticky liquid that made possible one of the world's most important inventions.

MANY PLANTS HAVE WAYS TO PREVENT INJURIES BECOMING INFECTED. Trees like frankincense and myrrh ooze pungent, antiseptic resin, while gutta-percha, like rubber (page 20) creates latex, a milky goo. Hundreds of years ago, tribespeople of the Malaysian rainforest discovered that, unlike rubber latex, once hardened in the air, gutta-percha could be softened again in hot water and molded into strong, waterproof items that would keep their shape.

IN 1843, A BRITISH DOCTOR STATIONED IN SINGAPORE WAS AMAZED TO SEE LOCALS WEARING WATERPROOF GUTTA-PERCHA OVERSHOES and carrying machetes with neatly-molded handles. He excitedly sent samples back to England, and soon businesses sprang up to exploit this new wonder material. Some companies used it to make unbreakable kitchenware—funnels, bowls, and food containers. Others sold chess pieces, furniture, toilet paper holders, and even shoes for animals. At that time, large lawns were sometimes mown by horse-drawn lawnmowers, but horses' hooves would kick up the turf, making unsightly marks. The solution: gutta-percha horses' bootees!

UNTIL THE MID-19TH CENTURY, ONLY VERY WEALTHY PEOPLE PLAYED GOLF, partly because golf balls were hand-stitched from leather and feathers, making them very expensive.

GUTTA-PERCHA BALLS, OR GUTTIES, were much cheaper, meaning more people could now play. Gutties were used for fifty years, until rubber eventually replaced gutta-percha.

IN THE 1850S, WERNER VON SIEMENS, A GERMAN INVENTOR LIVING IN LONDON, created something even more important than horse-bootees, gutties, and bathroom fittings. At that time, the only way to communicate instantaneously over long distances was by telegraph—a messaging technology that came before the telephone—which worked by sending electrical signals over long wires. Nobody had yet found a reliable way to make the telegraph work across the sea because water and electricity don't mix. Britain, being an island, was cut off from other countries.

AFTER MANY EXPERIMENTS, VON SIEMENS INVENTED THE FIRST WATERPROOF UNDERSEA CABLES using gutta-percha, which kept the wires dry and prevented them from touching each other. By the end of the 19th century, ships had laid undersea cables all over the world to carry telegraph messages and eventually, telephone calls. Gutta-percha's main use today is by dentists, who use it to fill the root of a tooth if it has become infected.

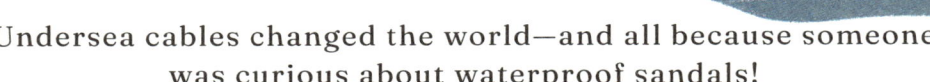

Undersea cables changed the world—and all because someone was curious about waterproof sandals!

Gutta-Percha
Palaquium gutta

This tropical tree's latex forms a protective skin over any wounds it receives, to keep out germs and discourage, or even trap, insects.

Gutta-percha trees produce a grayish **LATEX**, which can be extracted from crushed leaves or, like rubber, by making sloping cuts in the tree's bark and collecting the drips.

Eager for light, the tree **GROWS TALL AND STRAIGHT**, with branches and leaves only at its sunlit top.

Once it's exposed to the air, the **LATEX** turns yellow or pinkish and sets solid.

Its **LEAVES** are green and glossy when seen from above but beautiful bronze from below.

In spring, its little **WHITE FLOWERS** blossom close to the stems. They are followed in summer by edible brownish fruit the size of a plum—food for bats and macaques.

Corn, or Maize. There's much more to corn than popcorn or cornflakes. It is one of the most important crops in the world.

ABOUT 9,000 YEARS AGO, people living in the hills of Central America started to domesticate teosinte, a tiny wild grass with just a dozen or so little triangular seeds. It was first used for making beer and then to make flour for bread. Occasionally, farmers found a plant whose seeds were slightly sweeter, larger, or more plentiful than the others. They used the seeds of *that* teosinte for the next crop. When those seeds grew into plants, farmers again sowed seeds from the best ones. They repeated this over thousands of years.

EVENTUALLY, FARMERS BRED TEOSINTE INTO MAIZE, which has many large seeds, or kernels. Roasted, or made into bread, porridge, or beer, it soon became a staple food for the Inca people of Peru, the Maya of Central America, and the Aztecs of Mexico.

IT WAS SO IMPORTANT AS A FOOD CROP THAT PEOPLE WORSHIPPED THE PLANT, and placed gold and silver sculptures of maize in temples. The Incas cooked maize kernels in special three-legged stoves, heating them quickly so that steam trapped inside the tough little seed cases built up enough pressure to make each one explode. Ta-da! Popcorn! Aztec women wore popcorn necklaces to persuade the rain god Tlaloc to bring them more children, and fishermen threw popcorn into the sea to gain protection from the gods.

MEXICANS AND CENTRAL AMERICANS STILL ENJOY MANY KINDS OF MAIZE, with interesting flavors and often with brightly colored—sometimes even blue—seeds. Some farmers encourage a fungus called corn smut to infect the plant. It causes puffy, gray growths, called huitlacoche, which are an expensive delicacy with an earthy, smoky flavor.

MAIZE IS NOW GROWN WORLDWIDE, OVER A HUGE TOTAL AREA FOUR TIMES THE SIZE OF SPAIN! Most maize is grown for cattle feed or fermented to make alcohol for vehicle fuel. Only about a tenth of it is eaten by people, mostly as flour in foods like polenta and tortillas, or as corn syrup—a sugary substance added to many drinks, snack foods, and breakfast cereals. Cornflakes are made in factories—the husks are removed from the kernels, which are flavored with malt, sugar, and salt, then squashed between large steel rollers and toasted.

The best way to eat corn is straight from the cob—freshly picked, boiled, and buttered. Sweet!

Corn
Zea mays

Modern corn, which is also known as maize, towers high above our heads.

The **COBS**, or ears, can be as long as your forearm!

It takes two to three months for the cobs to grow, from planting to harvest.

Each cob contains about eight hundred plump **KERNELS**.

SOWN closely together, corn plants can form a living wall. Sometimes farmers do this for fun, and welcome visitors to their amazing maize mazes!

The **KERNELS** have been bred to stay on the cob, so corn is now dependent on humans to disperse its seed.

The biggest corn producers are the United States and China, where just a few bountiful varieties with uniform pale-yellow seeds are grown in enormous fields.

Dandelion. This modest little plant, which sends off its seeds in such a magnificent way, is beautiful and valuable, too.

DANDELIONS, RARELY MORE THAN ANKLE HEIGHT, grow throughout northern Europe, the United States and Canada. They dot the countryside and roadsides and often appear on garden lawns where they provide food for bees. Fussy gardeners might think of them as weeds and pull them out. In Europe, dandelion is a popular spring salad vegetable.

THE FRENCH MAKE A TANGY JELLY FROM DANDELION FLOWERS, and health-food stores sell dandelion "coffee," an almost-delicious caffeine-free brew made by roasting the plant's roots. Amazingly, dandelion roots have also contributed to heavy industry. If you pull up a dandelion and break or scrape a piece of the root, a sticky, milky-looking substance called latex appears at the wound.

The latex forms an airtight barrier against infection, while feeding insects are bogged down in the sticky sap and their mouthparts clog up.

Dandelion latex is very similar to the kind that is tapped from rubber trees, and can be processed and used in much the same way, in things like car and aircraft tires!

DURING WORLD WAR II, fighting interrupted the normal rubber supply from trees in Asia. Russia and the United States experimented with using **DANDELION RUBBER** instead. One species from Russia and Eastern Europe yielded much more rubber than others, and botanists used it to breed even better varieties. By the mid-1940s, hundreds of square miles of these dandelions had been planted in Eastern Europe. In North America, there were dandelion breeding programs and large-scale dandelion farms.

WHEN THE WAR ENDED IN 1945 and supplies returned to normal, dandelion rubber was forgotten for a while. Today, rubber is still vital for industry, and in order to prevent rainforests being chopped down to make way for plantations, people are searching for other sources. Unlike rubber trees, dandelions can easily grow in cool climates, and dandelion farming is reappearing in Europe.

Some modern car and truck tires contain dandelion rubber.

Dandelion
Taraxacum officinale

Dandelion flowers display a bull's eye pattern, which can only be seen under ultraviolet light. Invisible to us, it attracts bees.

Each **FLOWER HEAD** is composed of as many as two hundred tiny florets.

The most beautiful part of the dandelion is certainly not the root, nor even the flower, but the **SEED GLOBE**, or dandelion clock.

Dandelion **LEAVES** are good to eat, with a pleasant peppery taste. However, eating too many can make you want to pee!

The clock is a perfect sphere of **SEEDS**, each with its own minuscule parachute, ready to be blown by the wind . . .

. . . or by someone trying to tell the time, counting how many puffs it takes to make all the seeds fly away!

Prickly Pear. The prickly pear is entwined with Mexican culture and history. An Aztec legend of an eagle perched on the cactus even features on the Mexican flag.

TINY COCHINEAL BEETLES LIVE ON THE PLANT'S PRICKLY PADS. These beetles make a substance that deters birds and other insects from eating them, but which also happens to be a natural red dye. Over many centuries, the Aztecs and Maya of North and Central America learned to farm the beetles, transferring their eggs from plant to plant and harvesting the adults with a brush before drying and grinding them up. It takes more than 100,000 beetles to make two pounds of powdered red dye.

WHEN THE SPANISH ARRIVED IN MEXICO IN THE EARLY 1500S, they were astonished to see vivid red clothing and wall hangings that didn't fade in sunlight. Cochineal dye soon became a hugely profitable export to Europe, where it was used to make luxury scarlet clothing for royalty, nobles, and clergy—and became a sure sign of wealth and power.

IN THE 18TH CENTURY, AUSTRALIANS IMPORTED PRICKLY PEAR AND COCHINEAL BEETLES, hoping to make their own dye. But with no local herbivores, the cacti spread out of control and by the 1920s it covered large parts of Queensland and New South Wales, making an area the size of Britain unusable for grazing cattle. So, in 1926, biologists introduced the South American moth *Cactoblastis cactorum*, whose caterpillars enthusastically eat and destroy the cacti. Within just a few decades, Australia's prickly pear panic was over.

TODAY, ARTIFICIAL FABRIC DYES HAVE LARGELY REPLACED COCHINEAL, but it is still used in traditional textiles. It also makes carmine, a pigment that creates red and pink coloring in cosmetics, and food and drinks such as sausages, strawberry jam, and soft drinks.

With a tart taste and chewy texture, sliced prickly pear pads (with the spines removed!), known as nopalito in Mexico, are served boiled or grilled as a vegetable.

Prickly Pear
Opuntia ficus-indica

The prickly pear, the world's most common cactus, evolved to cope with very dry conditions.

The cactus stores precious water in plate-sized **PADS**—swollen stems with a waxy coating, guarded by ferocious spines. Unlike most other plants, cacti conserve moisture by opening their microscopic pores to absorb carbon dioxide only in the cool of the night. They convert it to more easily stored substances until the daytime, when sunlight provides the energy to use the food-store, and for the plant to grow.

Aztecs called the prickly pear nochtli, and associated it with the goddess of the sun. Its orange or yellow **FLOWERS** are bright bursts of color—nectar-filled beacons for feeding insects and birds.

The cactus's sweet, pear-shaped **FRUIT** changes color, from pale orange to deep purple as it ripens. Each one is protected by prickly clumps of barbed **HAIRS** that must be carefully removed if the fruit is to be eaten by people— they itch like mad!

The fruits eventually fall and split, attracting coyotes and crows to eat the flesh and disperse hundreds of small **SEEDS**.

Sugarcane. Sugarcane evolved in Southeast Asia, although today most of it is grown in Brazil and India. Three-quarters of the world's sugar comes from this one plant.

A METHOD FOR MAKING GRANULATED SUGAR FROM SUGARCANE JUICE WAS DISCOVERED IN INDIA NEARLY 2,000 YEARS AGO, and by 700 AD it had spread to the Islamic world.

IN THE MIDDLE AGES, SOLDIERS RETURNING TO EUROPE BROUGHT TINY AMOUNTS OF SUGAR HOME WITH THEM—but for ordinary people, honey continued to be their only sweetener. But in the 18th century, sugar became available and hugely popular. It was used to make sweets, chocolate, jams, cakes, and cookies, and to preserve food. Sugar helped to make tea, coffee, and cocoa more enjoyable, as it disguised the bitterness of substances that plants use to protect themselves from being eaten by insects and animals.

SUGAR WAS SUPPLIED FROM PLANTATIONS SET UP BY EUROPEANS IN THEIR COLONIES. These plantations depended on enslaved people transported to the Caribbean and Southern United States from West Africa. They were forced to do long hours of exhausting work, cutting the cane with heavy machetes, crushing it to extract the juices, and boiling it to create solid sugar.

TODAY, SUGAR PRODUCTION IS LARGELY MECHANIZED, but half of all sugarcane is still cut by hand before being crushed between heavy rollers to squeeze the juice. This is boiled down until solid raw sugar begins to crystallize, leaving behind thick, almost-black molasses that tastes like smoky caramel and burnt toffee. Yum!

RAW SUGAR IS REFINED TO MAKE DIFFERENT SOLID SUGARS. The darkest, meltiest muscovado has the strongest taste and is perfect for porridge. Mid-brown demerara sugar suits coffee. Pure white sugar, sweet but otherwise tasteless, is used in candies, jams, and drinks, and added to many foods to make them more appealing.

WHY DO SUGARY THINGS TASTE SO GOOD? Many plants evolved to produce sweet, energy-giving fruits that attract animals to eat them. In return, the plant's seeds are spread in the animals' poo.

Humans, too, have evolved to associate sweet flavor with nourishment. That's why, although we know that too much sugar is bad for our health, it's hard to resist.

Sugarcane
Saccharum officinarum

Sugarcane is a giant grass that grows best near the equator, as it needs plenty of light and heat, as well as water.

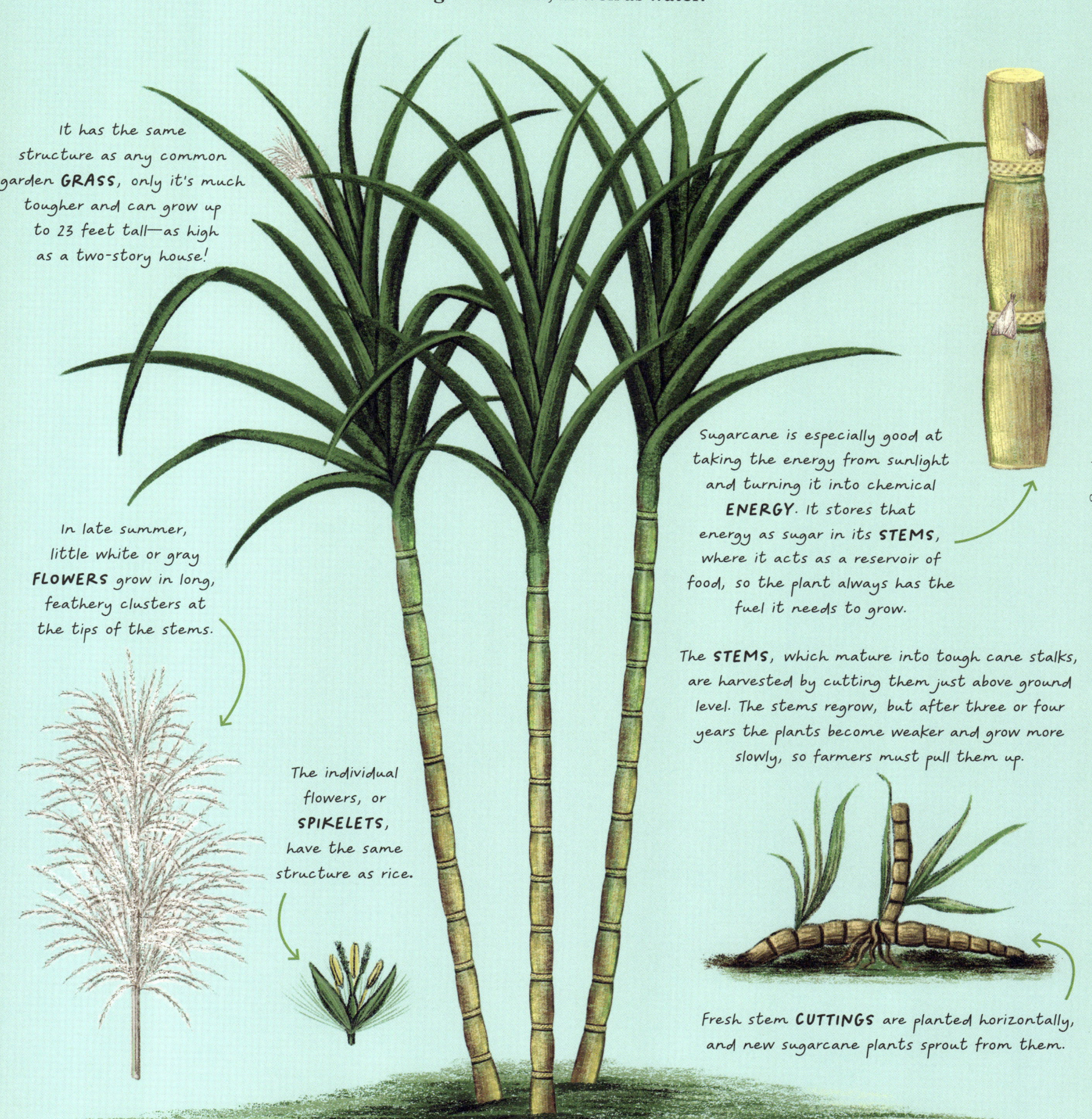

It has the same structure as any common garden **GRASS**, only it's much tougher and can grow up to 23 feet tall—as high as a two-story house!

In late summer, little white or gray **FLOWERS** grow in long, feathery clusters at the tips of the stems.

The individual flowers, or **SPIKELETS**, have the same structure as rice.

Sugarcane is especially good at taking the energy from sunlight and turning it into chemical **ENERGY**. It stores that energy as sugar in its **STEMS**, where it acts as a reservoir of food, so the plant always has the fuel it needs to grow.

The **STEMS**, which mature into tough cane stalks, are harvested by cutting them just above ground level. The stems regrow, but after three or four years the plants become weaker and grow more slowly, so farmers must pull them up.

Fresh stem **CUTTINGS** are planted horizontally, and new sugarcane plants sprout from them.

Pumpkin. People in South America began to breed and cultivate squash 8,000 years ago. Worldwide, there are now countless varieties suited to local climates and tastes.

THE MAYA OF ANCIENT MEXICO AND CENTRAL AMERICA developed a clever way to grow their main crop plants of squash, beans, and maize. They noticed that the crops did best when they were planted together, rather than in separate fields of their own.

BEANS are very nutritious but can also use the bacteria living in their roots to feed the soil with fertilizer. **CORN** uses that fertilizer to grow tall. The tall corn supports climbing beans and squash. The **SQUASH** forms a green blanket over the ground that prevents weeds from growing, stops precious water from evaporating, and even stops wind and rain from wearing away the soil.

WHAT A TEAM! Native Americans called this system "the three sisters" because the squash, beans, and corn seem to look after each other.

THE PUMPKIN IS CELEBRATED FOR ITS CONNECTION WITH HALLOWEEN, a festival at the end of October, full of pranks and mischief, sweets and costumes. The charming Halloween tradition of placing candles inside carved lanterns began in Europe with turnips—they must have been rather small! Casting their orange glow, popular pumpkin lantern designs feature bats, cats and grinning faces.

The closely related **GIANT PUMPKIN** (*Cucurbita maxima*) can grow ludicrously big. The world record is more than 2,000 pounds, the weight of a small car. They're the world's heaviest fruit, but they're far too watery and bland to eat.

Giant pumpkins can be so big they can be hollowed out and used for pumpkin-boat races—possibly the most delightfully ridiculous sport in the world!

Pumpkin
The cucurbit family

A pumpkin is a kind of squash. But is it a fruit or a vegetable? They're not very sweet, so most people think pumpkins are vegetables. But because they have seeds and develop from a flower, they are actually fruits.

PUMPKIN is a general name for any of the fruits in the squash (or cucurbit) family that look big, round, and orange.

Squashes are fiesty, fast-growing plants with big, bold **LEAVES** and showy yellow or orange **FLOWERS**.

The **FRUITS** of the cucurbit family come in a carnival of shapes and colors, and range in size from miniature apple-sized squashes to giant pumpkins.

Pumpkin **VINES** scramble over the ground and clamber up poles and other plants, clinging to them with their tough tendrils.

Nutmeg. Until the 19th century, the Banda Islands—small volcanic islands now part of Indonesia—were the only place in the world where nutmeg grew.

THE SPICE REACHED INDIA MORE THAN 2,500 YEARS AGO and was also used by ancient Egyptians but didn't arrive in Europe until the 13th century. Nutmeg's warm and exotic flavor made it an immediate hit and extremely valuable. Its Arab traders managed to keep the source secret for nearly two hundred years.

EVENTUALLY EUROPEANS DISCOVERED THE SOURCE and the Dutch, British, and French began fighting to gain control of the plantations. The nutmeg trade became especially lucrative when rumors spread that, as well as being an exotic and tasty spice, it could prevent or even cure plague. In the 16th century, plague doctors wore protective capes and masks with a "breathing beak" that held spices, including nutmeg, thought to purify the air.

EARLY IN THE 17TH CENTURY, the British acquired a major source of nutmeg—the island of Rhun—but the Dutch forced them out. Finally, in 1667, they came to a deal—the Dutch swapped Rhun for Manhatten, their American colony, known then as New Amsterdam. The British renamed it New York.

EVENTUALLY, THE FRENCH BOTANIST, PIERRE POIVRE, managed to smuggle some nutmeg seeds to Mauritius, where it was planted, finally breaking Dutch control of nutmeg cultivation.

NUTMEG WAS VALUABLE BECAUSE IT WAS ONLY GROWN IN ONE PLACE AND MANY PEOPLE WANTED IT. It was also more than just a delicious way to make bland food more interesting. People believed it brought good luck, prevented diseases, and even made people fall in love with each other!

IN THE 18TH CENTURY, IT WAS THE FASHION FOR MEN TO CARRY POCKET NUTMEG GRATERS—with a special little compartment for the seed itself—so they could readily add the spice to food and drink.

MACE IS THE SPICE MADE from the red covering of the nutmeg seed. It is terrific with fruit, in soups and stews, and for baking, while the slightly more pungent nutmeg can be grated onto potatoes, cauliflower, and spinach, and is especially good in milky drinks and rice pudding.

Nutmeg should always be added at the very end of cooking, to preserve its flavor.

Nutmeg
Myristica fragrans

The nutmeg tree yields two delicious and valuable spices.

The fragrance of nutmeg's little pale yellow **BLOSSOMS** attracts tiny beetles, flies, and thrips, insects that can squeeze inside their narrow openings and carry pollen from flower to flower.

Each tree produces hundreds of yellow **FRUITS** the size of a small apple.

As the fruits ripen, they **SPLIT** to reveal a tough seed case, cloaked in a lacy scarlet covering, or aril. If farmers don't get there first, nutmeg pigeons gobble the bright aril and discard the seeds. This aril, which dries to a yellowish-brown, is the spice known as **MACE**.

The mace surrounding the **SEEDS** is separated, sun-dried, and sold. The remaining seed cases are cracked by machines—the kernel inside each one is the nutmeg. Grating nutmeg reveals a pleasing pattern of vessels that contain warming, fragrant oils.

Henna. Henna has been used as a decorative hair and skin dye for thousands of years by many different cultures.

WHILE HENNA FLOWERS HAVE A DELIGHTFUL SCENT, the plant's special trick is the dye that can be extracted from its leaves. Henna is grown in fields and harvested once the plants are about shoulder high, traditionally with a sickle in one hand and a tough glove on the other. The leaves are stripped and dried in the sun, before being ground into a dull-looking green powder that's exported all over the world.

WHEN THE POWDER IS MIXED TO A PASTE WITH WATER AND A LITTLE LEMON JUICE, a chemical called lawsone is released. Within the henna plant it kills germs and deters insect pests. But fortunately for us, it also makes an excellent dye. Lawsone not only produces a pleasing, warm orangey-brown color on fabrics but works especially well on human hair and skin, too.

IN THE MIDDLE EAST AND SOUTH ASIA, older men sometimes use henna to dye their gray beards orange, but most henna is used by women. It gives a glorious auburn sheen to black hair, while appearing boldly orange or reddish-brown on hair that is blonde or gray. Sometimes a little black tea is added to the henna to adjust the color.

HENNA IS COMMONLY USED BY HINDU AND MUSLIM WOMEN FOR TEMPORARY TATTOOS, or body art, for special occasions. The henna paste is squeezed through a fine nozzle or painted onto the skin in intricate and beautiful patterns, most frequently on the hands and feet but sometimes on the arms and even faces, too. For the dye to take effect, the lines of paste must be left for several hours before being washed off to reveal designs that gradually darken in color from orange to dark brown, before fading over a few weeks.

THE BEST PLACE TO SEE HENNA DECORATION IS AT A HINDU OR MUSLIM WEDDING. The evening before, there is a mehndi (henna) party with music and dancing, where women apply elaborate patterns to the bride, and each other, to celebrate and bring good luck.

India is the world's largest producer of henna—and most of it comes from Rajasthan, a state in the arid northwest of the country, also known for its medieval forts.

Henna

Lawsonia inermis

Henna is a shrub or small tree that is native to North Africa, the Middle East, and the parts of South Asia with a dry climate and plenty of sunshine.

Henna's slender, branching stems are covered in thumb-sized oval **LEAVES**. Although they might not seem very special, they are the most valuable part of the plant, as this is where the precious dye comes from.

After flowering, henna's **SEEDS** are contained in pretty sprays of purple or reddish berries.

Tiny cream or pale-pink **FLOWERS** bloom in clusters, and are deliciously fragrant, reminiscent of jasmine or rose.

Henna is much tougher than it looks. Even when it has shriveled from lack of rain and appears to be quite dead, it can spring back to life with just a little water.

A precious **OIL** extracted from the flowers, called attar of henna, is used to add a warm and spicy scent to some perfumes.

Rice. Rice feeds more people than any other crop. The grain has been cultivated in China and northern India for around 11,000 years and most of it is still grown in Asia, where it is a staple food for billions of people.

RICE HAS A LONG HISTORY, WITH MANY TRADITIONS, and it often symbolizes abundance and prosperity. In South India, during the annual Pongal harvest festival in mid-January, people give thanks by serving a special dish made with freshly grown rice, milk, and raw sugar. It's cooked in a clay pot until it overflows, promising good fortune for the coming year.

In many countries, rice is thrown over the bride and groom at weddings, in the hope that they in turn will be showered with children, wealth, and happiness.

AFTER HARVESTING, THE RICE GRAIN IS SEPARATED FROM THE STALKS and indigestible seed casings and, to prevent mold, quickly dried. This process produces simple brown or whole grain rice. To make white rice, parts of the grain are removed. Brown rice is a much healthier food, as it contains more protein and vitamins, but white rice is often preferred for its taste, its fast cooking time, and longer shelf life.

THERE ARE THOUSANDS OF VARIETIES OF RICE, with different colors, shapes, tastes, and cooking qualities. Some, such as Basmati, have long grains that stay separate. Others, with shorter grains, clump together and are perfect for sushi or sticky rice. Short-grain Arborio remains a little chewy, making it ideal for risotto and puddings.

WHEN BUILDINGS ARE CONSTRUCTED FROM BRICK OR STONE, a paste of sand, water, and limestone, known as mortar, is used to fill the gaps. It acts like glue, making the structure stable. Around 1,600 years ago, Chinese builders discovered that adding a little soup of sticky rice to mortar made it less runny, finer, and longer lasting. Sticky rice mortar was used to build palaces, tombs, and temples, and sections of the Great Wall of China.

Rice is such a big part of the culture that in many Southeast Asian countries people sometimes greet each other with words that literally mean "Have you eaten rice today?"

Rice
Oryza sativa

Rice is a grass with multiple stalks, each bearing clusters of tiny flowers.

Rice evolved to survive in tropical areas that were flooded from time to time. Rice still grows best in flat fields, or **PADDIES**, that have around an inch of water for most of the year.

RICE FLOWERS have no need to be brightly colored or scented to attract insects, as their pollen is instead carried by the breeze.

Hollow chambers in the **STEMS** allow air from **PORES** in the leaves to travel down through the plant and eventually to the **ROOTS**, enabling rice to thrive in waterlogged soil.

The seeds of the rice plant, known as **GRAINS**, contain plenty of stored food for the new plant to be able to grow. This makes rice, along with other grass grains, such as wheat and oats, one of the world's most important sources of carbohydrates.

When the grains are almost ripe, the paddy fields are drained so that the stalks, along with the grains, can be **HARVESTED**.

Black Pepper. Freshly ground black pepper isn't just spicy hot, but deliciously aromatic, too. Used around the world, this spice stimulates the stomach and literally makes the mouth water.

TODAY, MORE THAN A THIRD OF ALL BLACK PEPPER COMES FROM VIETNAM, but it originated in southwestern India, where it is still grown today.

IN ANCIENT ROME, pepper was a vital ingredient in medicines as well as cooking, but it was an expensive luxury. Nearly 2,000 years ago, Indian writers described fine ships arriving with Roman gold and leaving laden with pepper.

IN THE MIDDLE AGES, WEALTHY EUROPEANS WERE CRAZY FOR PEPPER. It made bland food exciting and was also thought to warm the body, dry up colds, and reduce burping and farting. The journey to Europe involved costly sea voyages, slow overland camel caravans, and paying many middlemen along the way. Its high value and exotic origin made pepper a symbol of status and power. Peppercorns were easily counted and valuable enough to be used as money.

THE TRADE IN SPICES ENCOURAGED EUROPEANS TO EXPLORE THE WORLD. The first contact between Europe, the Caribbean, and North America was inspired by the search for an easy sea route to India. And when Vasco da Gama sailed from Portugal all the way around Africa, arriving in India in 1498, his purpose was pepper. For hundreds of years European powers competed, and even fought, for spices. Over the centuries, as new sources of pepper were discovered or planted, its price dropped, and more people could enjoy it. In many countries, it can now be found on almost every dinner table.

SOME OF THE FLAVORS IN BLACK PEPPER ARE DESTROYED BY LIGHT AND HEAT, so it should be kept in the dark and ground into food just before eating. The first table pepper grinders were sold in 1874 by Peugeot, a French family firm that later made motor cars.

When the Egyptian pharaoh Rameses the Great was mummified in 1213 BC, peppercorns were placed in his nostrils! Nobody knows exactly how they arrived in Egypt from India.

Black Pepper
Piper nigrum

The black pepper plant is a climbing vine that scrambles enthusiastically up forest trees or tall farmers' poles.

Its shiny dark-green **LEAVES** smell temptingly of pepper when they're crushed.

Blossoming with the arrival of monsoon rains, clusters of minuscule cream or yellow-green **FLOWERS** are strung out along stalks that hang like catkins.

The precious little **FRUIT**, known as a peppercorn, resembles a small berry and contains a single seed. The stalks, each bearing a few dozen peppercorns, are collected by farmers, who stand on ladders to harvest them by hand. New pepper plants are grown from cuttings, although in the wild, birds swallow and disperse the seeds.

The pungent spice known as black pepper is made by leaving shiny, green, slightly **UNRIPE FRUIT** to dry and wrinkle in the sun for a few days. If the fruits are picked once they turn a little red, and soaked for a week, their outer layer can be rubbed away to reveal milder white pepper.

Beech. Tall, majestic beech trees are a familiar sight in parks and woodlands across Europe. They have a fascinating history.

THUNDERSTORMS USUALLY BRING PLENTY OF RAIN. If a beech tree is stuck by lightning, electricity can often flow harmlessly along the film of rainwater that sits on the tree's smooth bark, and down to the ground. A natural lightning conductor! Other kids of trees with craggy bark have dry patches where the rain can't reach, so electricity from lightning is more likely to flow through the moist heart of the tree, causing the water inside to boil. Bang!

THE ABILITY TO SURVIVE LIGHTNING HAS LED MANY CULTURES TO ASSOCIATE BEECH TREES WITH THUNDERSTORMS. For the Teutons, an ancient Germanic tribe, the beech was sacred to Thor, the god of thunder. In England, people once believed that beechwood could protect their homes against lightning, and Germans still have a saying that lightning never strikes a beech tree. In fact, they are hit just as often as other tall trees, but their smooth bark helps keep them safe.

BEECH TIMBER IS AN ATTRACTIVE LIGHT-STRAW COLOR. 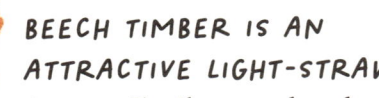 Easily sawed and carved, it can also be softened with steam and bent into various shapes, so it is often used to make tool handles, kitchen spoons and spatulas, toys, and chairs. Desktops and doors are often made of cheaper materials and then clad in a beautiful, thin layer, or veneer, of beechwood, which is glued to the surface. Veneers are made by stripping the bark from logs, steaming the wood to soften it, and peeling a continuous thin layer of bark as the log is turned against a long, sharp blade. Layers of veneer can be glued on top of each other to make plywood, a very strong material used to make roofs, floors, and even the walls of houses.

HOWEVER, THE SMOOTH BARK OF BEECH TREES MAKES THEM VULNERABLE to people who carve messages or love hearts into the bark—graffiti that can last for decades.

Old beech forests are strangely quiet places. The usual rustle of undergrowth is missing, and when the leaves fall, they form a carpet that muffles sound. Shhh!

Beech
Fagus sylvatica

The beech tree's smooth bark helps to protect it from lightning.

Beech **LEAVES** have diagonal patterning and crinkled edges. When they're young, a layer of silken hairs helps to prevent them from drying out.

The leaves darken as they mature, putting on a gorgeous autumn display of gold and bronze before the tree sheds for the winter.

MALE BEECH FLOWERS are stubby, shaggy little catkins on long stalks.

Their pollen floats on the wind to **FEMALE FLOWERS**, nestling in little cups that look like miniature lime-green or pink mops.

The cups eventually become woody to protect their **NUTS** inside, which are known as beechmast and provide food for many birds and mammals.

Beech **BARK** is unusual. It continually sheds its top layer, allowing it to expand as the tree grows. The fresh bark is thin but curiously smooth.

Some say their smooth gray **TRUNKS** and trunk flares look like elephant legs and feet!

Olive. Olive trees first grew in the eastern Mediterranean and have been cultivated for more than 5,000 years.

ROMANS OFTEN CLEANED THEMSELVES BY RUBBING OLIVE OIL INTO THEIR SKIN and then scraping it off, together with any dirt, using a strigil, a curved metal blade.

TO ANCIENT EGYPTIANS, GREEKS, JEWS AND ROMANS, OLIVE OIL WAS LIQUID GOLD. They used it for cooking, religious ceremonies, and anointing priests and kings. Thousands of years before electric light was invented, it was the brightly burning fuel for lamps.

AT THE ANCIENT OLYMPIC GAMES HELD IN GREECE SOME 2,500 YEARS AGO, the winners were crowned with an olive wreath, or kotinos, the equivalent of a gold medal today.

THE OLIVE BRANCH HAS BEEN A SYMBOL OF PEACE AND FRIENDSHIP SINCE ANCIENT TIMES. In the Bible story of Noah's Ark, a dove brought an olive branch to show the great flood had eased. Today, the United Nations flag shows a map of the world surrounded by olive branches.

MOST OLIVES TODAY ARE GROWN FOR THEIR DELICIOUS OIL, which is made when the fruit is fully ripe in late autumn or early winter. Farmers harvest the olives by shaking the branches and catching them on mats beneath the trees. Large machines then wash and crush the olives without breaking the stones, and the oil is separated from the flesh and any juice in a process called pressing. The first cold press produces virgin olive oil. Further pressings, each a little warmer and eventually with hot water, extract more oil, which is a little less tasty each time.

WHEN OLIVES ARE PICKED UNRIPE, THEY ARE GREEN. WHEN THEY ARE FULLY RIPE THEY ARE BLACK. Either way, straight from the tree, they taste appallingly bitter. To prepare them for eating they're pickled in brine for several months, often along with herbs and spices. The transformation is magical! Every culture has its favorite olive varieties and special ways of preparing them.

Some olive trees are certainly more than a thousand years old, but how much more is hard to know. The trees often become hollow with age, preventing rings from being counted.

Olive
Olea europaea

There are about 150 commonly planted varieties of olive, such as picual, kalamata, and manzanilla.

Olive trees need at least two months of cold winter weather, below 50°F, before they can grow their tiny white **FLOWERS** in spring and a crop of **FRUIT**—olives!—in summer.

Olive trees have adapted to survive hot, dry summers. Their narrow, leathery leaves are dusty green on top but silvery underneath due to microscopic overlapping **SCALES** that reduce water loss in extreme heat and wind.

A hard pit, or stone, in each olive contains a **SEED**.

Deep, spreading **ROOTS** help them to manage with very little rain.

In summer and autumn they ripen, turning from green to blue-black.

Wheat. Wheat was one of the first plants to be bred and grown by humans.

THE GRASSES THAT WERE THE ANCESTORS OF MODERN WHEAT GREW IN THE FERTILE CRESCENT, an area between the eastern Mediterranean and what is now Iran and Iraq. About 12,000 years ago, people began growing the seeds from the best plants. Over time, wheat became taller, more nutritious, and easier to grow in different climates.

AS PEOPLE BECAME LESS NOMADIC AND STAYED IN ONE PLACE, they began to plant, tend, and harvest wheat, and distribute the grain. Towns and cities began to grow.

TODAY, VARIETIES OF WHEAT HAVE BEEN BRED THAT CAN THRIVE IN THE HEAT AND COLD, AND ON EVERY CONTINENT EXCEPT ANTARCTICA. Wheat is planted on more land than any other crop. Most of it is milled to make flour for bread, cakes, and pastries, and it is also the main ingredient in pasta and many breakfast cereals.

WHOLE WHEAT IS A VERY HEALTHY FOOD. It contains carbohydrate, protein, fiber, vitamins, and minerals. Some of the proteins in wheat combine to form gluten. When flour and water are mixed to make dough, it is the gluten that makes it elastic when it is kneaded and chewy when it is cooked. If yeast, a simple fungus, is added to the dough, it feeds on natural sugars in the flour and makes carbon dioxide gas. Tiny bubbles of gas trapped by the gluten cause the dough to expand, or rise. In the heat of the oven, the gas expands even more, making even bigger bubbles and a larger, lighter loaf, which sets as it cooks.

IN MEDIEVAL TIMES, FRUMENTY—a popular porridge made from lightly crushed new wheat soaked in hot water or milk—was eaten with honey or fruit, or something savory for supper. In parts of Europe, as much wheat was used for making frumenty as for bread.

TO MAKE WHITE FLOUR, PARTS OF THE WHEAT GRAIN ARE REMOVED. White flour has a longer shelf life and some people prefer the flavor and texture of bread that is made from it, but wholemeal flour is much more nutritious.

Freshly harvested wheat must be threshed, to separate the grain from the stalks, and winnowed, to remove the indigestible seed casings—the chaff.

Wheat
Triticum aestivum

Like rice, oats, and barley, wheat is a grass widely cultivated for its edible seeds, known as grain.

Each plant has a handful of slender, hollow **STEMS**, which usually grow to about the height of a chair. The dried stems can be used to make thatched roofs.

Wild grasses ripen at different times and easily scatter their **SEEDS** on the ground once they're mature. The seeds take root where they land, or are transported by animals on their fur or in their poo.

Humans have bred wheat so that all the plants in a crop ripen at the same time and also hang on to their seeds. This way, whole fields can be harvested easily and in one go, but it does mean that modern wheat depends on humans to be able to reproduce.

At the top of each stem is the **EAR**, or **HEAD**—clusters of tiny **FLOWERS**, each of which becomes a hard grain that turns golden-yellow when ripe.

Wheat is an annual plant, meaning it only survives one growing season and must be planted anew for each crop.

Baobab. Baobabs, dotted across the bushland of most of southern Africa, are among the world's largest flowering plants.

THEY ARE ALSO AMONG THE LONGEST LIVED— each tree can survive for more than 2,000 years! Often solitary, they serve as landmarks over many human generations, and provide food and lodging for mammals and insects, reptiles and birds. Thirsty elephants sometimes visit to plunder baobab trees, ripping off pieces of bark to get to the water stored inside.

PLENTY OF FOLKTALES ACCOUNT FOR THE BAOBAB'S ODD LOOK, with its stubby, often leafless branches. A common theme is that the tree had "lofty ideas" and after much to-ing and fro-ing, the Creator, exasperated, flung the baobab upside down, leaving its roots in the air!

BAOBABS ARE OFTEN HOLLOW, a result of fungal infections, or because a ring of several nearby stems have fused together to make one big trunk. They have been used as storehouses, tombs, and, occasionally, temporary prisons!

THE BAOBAB HAS MANY OTHER USES. The powdery pulp of its fruit, pleasingly tart and bursting with vitamin C, is mixed with water or milk to make a refreshing drink, or added to maize porridge. Its seeds can be roasted and eaten like nuts, or pressed for their oil, which is also used in cosmetics. Its leaves, which are nutritious, tasty, and slightly sour, are popular raw in salads or cooked as a vegetable.

BAOBAB BARK CONTAINS STRONG FIBER that is used for making rope, handbags, and hats, or for weaving into cloth. Fortunately, the baobab is one of the few trees whose bark regenerates after it has been stripped.

A COMMON SUPERSTITION ACROSS THE AFRICAN CONTINENT IS THAT THE SOULS OF ANCESTORS INHABIT BAOBAB TREES. The indigenous San people of southern Africa sometimes say that any person who plucks the baobab's flowers will disturb the spirits and be chased by lions.

Baobabs are useful, but often considered sacred, too, making them even more likely to be protected.

Baobab
Adansonia digitata

The baobab is often called the elephant tree. Smooth and gray, its massive, pulpy trunk can store thousands of liters of water, and grows and shrinks with rainfall or in drought.

The baobab is famous for its massive **TRUNK**. With a circumference that can be more than 130 feet, at least eighteen adults would need to hold hands to surround it!

In the dry season, baobabs conserve water by dropping their **LEAVES**. They remain leafless for eight months of the year, contributing to their strange appearance.

At dusk, the baobab's spectacular floppy white **FLOWERS** open so fast that you can watch the petals unfurl. Whiffing of rotten meat, they dangle upside down on long, sturdy stems and produce sweet nectar, attracting and rewarding the tree's main pollinator, the nocturnal **FRUIT BAT**.

The tree's hefty oval **FRUIT** hang from long stalks like giant light pulls. Their khaki shells are velvet to the touch and conceal powdery beige flesh with dozens of large **SEEDS**, which are dispersed over long distances by elephants and baboons.

Tomato. Crop scientists believe that the ancestors of tomatoes were tiny berries growing wild on straggly vines near the coast of what is now Ecuador and Venezuela.

INDIGENOUS PEOPLE PROBABLY BRED TOMATOES INTO CHERRY-SIZED FRUIT, which were either brought by traders or carried by birds to Central America. There, they eventually became the fruit that was known to Maya people as tomatl (which translates to "plump thing"). When the Spanish arrived in 1519, they described seeing many different shapes and colors of tomatoes, and they brought them back to Europe.

ALTHOUGH TOMATOES ARE MEMBERS OF THE OFTEN-TOXIC NIGHTSHADE FAMILY, southern Europeans soon found them to be safe and appetizing. However, at the end of the 16th century, John Gerard, an influential English herbalist, remained suspicious. He described tomatoes as inedible and "of rank and stinking savour," despite knowing that Italians and Spaniards were enjoying them! As a result, people in Britain and North America mostly planted tomatoes for decoration and were put off eating them for about two hundred years.

TOMATOES ARE OFTEN HARVESTED AND TRANSPORTED WHEN THEY ARE HARD AND GREEN, AND LESS EASILY DAMAGED. They can later be exposed to ethylene, a gas that triggers fruit ripening. However, tomatoes are much tastier when they have been allowed to ripen naturally on the vine. And incredibly, researchers in South Korea discovered that playing a loud high-C whistle for about six hours can delay the ripening of harvested tomatoes by nearly a week! The sound vibrations seem to interfere with the fruit's own natural production of ethylene.

MILLIONS OF BOTTLES OF TOMATO KETCHUP ARE CONSUMED EVERY DAY. It's made by pulping ripe tomatoes, mixing them with sugar, vinegar, water, salt, and spices, and cooking at around 195°F. Xanthan gum is often added to thicken the ketchup and keep the ingredients from separating when they're stored. It also gives ketchup the curious property of becoming runnier the more its bottle is shaken (with the lid on!).

At the annual festival of La Tomatina in Buñol, southern Spain, some 20,000 people hurl overripe tomatoes at each other. Using fruit that would have otherwise gone to waste, it is the biggest, and messiest, food fight in the world.

Tomato

Solanum lycopersicum

Although we use it as a vegetable, the tomato is in fact a fruit.

The tomato plant is a small bush or climbing vine. Its **LEAVES** and **STEMS** have a tangy, grassy scent and are cloaked in short, fine hairs called **TRICHOMES**. They create an obstacle course for feeding insects and contain substances that deter insects and even lure their pests' enemies.

To release their pollen, the tomato's cheerful yellow **FLOWERS** must be shaken, either by wind or by bees, who cling tight and "buzz-pollinate" them by vibrating their bodies. Where tomatoes are grown in large windless greenhouses, bumblebee colonies are often kept on standby to do this job.

In the **FRUIT,** tomato **SEEDS** sit in a runny jelly, which some people find a little slimy. Most tomatoes ripen to vivid red, but varieties range from golden-yellow to the blackest purple and vary in size from a cherry to a bowling ball!

Unlike the tomato's mouthwatering fruit, its **LEAVES** are well defended with poisons— so don't eat them!

Coconut. Nothing says "tropical paradise" quite like gently swaying coconut palms. But these wonder plants are extraordinarily useful, too.

THE HUSK—THE OUTER LAYER OF THE FRUIT—IS COMPOSED OF COCONUT FIBER, OR COIR. It is used to make brooms, brushes, and doormats, to stuff mattresses and for ropes that conveniently float in water. When coconuts are exported, the husk is often removed to save space, exposing the tough brown shell underneath.

COCONUT SHELL IS USED FOR FUEL, or cut and glued to make jewelry, ornaments, bowls, and dishes. Pairs of empty shell halves were used in the early days of radio to simulate the clip-clopping sound of horses' hooves. Try it!

THE EDIBLE WHITE FLESH IS KNOWN AS COCONUT MEAT AND CAN BE EATEN RAW OR USED IN COOKING. Dried coconut meat, or copra, is used for its oil. Copra's chemistry and high fat content mean that in damp conditions it may self-heat or even catch fire, so there are special regulations for transporting it on ships, and it is banned from most airlines.

ACTIVATED CARBON, a substance made from granules of coconut shell that have been heated to make charcoal, is used in the air filters aboard the International Space Station. It purifies the air and absorbs toilet smells and astronauts' farts.

WATERPROOF PALM FRONDS ARE USED FOR THATCHING ROOFS, and individual leaflets can be braided or woven into mats and baskets. The trunks of coconut palms are used to construct small buildings and bridges, while the sweet sap from its flower stalks can be boiled down to make jaggery—a rough, dark sugar. Oh— and of course!— coconut water is a delicious thirst-quenching drink and coconut milk a tasty, high-fat food.

Many cultures celebrate the life-giving qualities of this incredibly useful tree. Coconuts are an offering in Hindu weddings, festivals, and religious rituals, and in Polynesian mythology, the universe itself emerged from a coconut.

Coconut
Cocos nucifera

Coconut palms only grow in the tropics, the hot and humid regions near to the equator. Although they can weather a typhoon, they cannot survive frost.

The **COMMON NAMES** given to coconut palms signal their importance. In the Philippines, for example, they are the "tree of life". In India, they're the "tree that fulfills all wishes" and in Malaysia, the "tree of a thousand uses."

Ripe coconuts have an outer husk consisting of a waterproof, yellowish-green skin surrounding a thick layer of fiber (coir) that traps air, enabling the **FRUIT** to float.

Coconut palms grow up to 100 feet tall and are topped with a few dozen **LEAVES**, or fronds. To prevent the tree from being uprooted in high wind, the fronds can bend backward into a more aerodynamic shape.

OUTER SKIN

COCONUT WATER

COIR

COCONUT MEAT (COPRA)

SHELL

Clusters of **FLOWERS** grow on long stems in the boughs of the coconut tree—a few males and a larger number of bigger, female flowers, which develop into coconut fruit—each one the size of a child's head!

Inside, a hard brown shell contains sweet coconut water. As the coconut ripens, a jelly-like layer forms on the inside of the shell and gradually solidifies to become white **COCONUT MEAT**.

Coconut palms tolerate salt and are one of the few plants that can take root on shorelines after **SEEDS** have floated there on the sea.

Peanut. Peanuts originated in South America and are now grown in many countries with warm climates, especially China, India, Nigeria, and the Southern United States. There are many reasons why they're so popular.

PEANUTS ARE AN ESPECIALLY TASTY AND NUTRITIOUS FOOD, as they contain plenty of protein, fiber, and vitamins, and a lot of oil. They can be eaten whole or ground up to make peanut butter.

They're used to make SAVORY SATAY SAUCES in Indonesia...

...PEANUT BUTTER AND JELLY SANDWICHES and MILKSHAKES in the US...

...and SOUPS and STEWS in West Africa.

THE SEED PODS ARE HARVESTED USING A SPECIAL DIGGER to pull up the plant and flip it upside down to dry for a few days, before a mechanical stripper separates out the peanut pods. After cleaning and removing them from their pods, peanuts are roasted to kill any germs and bring out their flavor.

TO EXTRACT THE OIL, PEANUTS ARE FLAKED AND SQUEEZED IN A POWERFUL PRESS, and the leftover "cake" makes excellent cattle feed. The oil is further purified and used for cooking because it has a light flavor and withstands high heat. Peanut oil is also made into margarine and is even used as a raw material in paints and cosmetics.

PEANUT BUTTER, KNOWN TO THE INCA OF SOUTH AMERICA THOUSANDS OF YEARS AGO, became popular in the United States in the late 19th century when machines were invented to make large batches. In 1895, Dr. John Kellogg (yes, the man who invented cornflakes!) developed a peanut paste that could be "cut up in thin or thick slices, like cheese". Agricultural scientist George Washington Carver researched peanut cultivation, and he and other inventors worked on different machines to turn peanuts into spreads and food supplements. Today, clean, roasted peanuts on wire grids are jiggled in jets of air to blow away the skins, then chopped with rotating blades to form a smooth butter. Other ingredients are sometimes added, such as sugar, or palm oil, which prevents the peanut oil and solids from separating.

Even though it needs stirring occasionally to mix the oil by hand, the best peanut butter (crunchy, please!) contains *only* peanuts and a little salt.

Peanut
Arachis hypogaea

This low and bushy plant seems quite ordinary but there is something very clever and unusual about this common plant.

The peanut plant's leaves close at night, and each of its orange or yellow **FLOWERS**, shaped like a little butterfly, blooms for just one day.

After the flowers are pollinated, the peanut plant does something rare and marvelous. Each flower stalk turns downward and keeps growing, pushing the developing seed pod, which is its **FRUIT**, straight into the soil!

When the stalk reaches a finger's depth beneath the soil, it stops and turns sideways.

The peanut plant plants its own **SEED**!

The **POD**, usually with two seeds (peanuts) in a fibrous shell, develops underground, well protected from foraging animals.

Peanuts are not true nuts but are legumes, a large family of plants that includes beans, chickpeas, and peas, as well as henna.

Friendly bacteria that live in their **ROOTS** enable them to make their own fertilizer from nitrogen in the air, putting goodness back in the soil.

I dedicate this book to people who celebrate curiosity and ask LOTS of questions!—Jonathan Drori

Glossary

COLONIZATION: Taking control over indigenous land and people, often for economic benefit.

CULTIVATE: To prepare the land and grow, tend, and harvest plants.

ECOSYSTEM: A community of living organisms—plants, animals, and microbes—in a particular area.

EVERGREEN: A plant that has green leaves throughout the year.

EVOLVE: To change or adapt over time into a form more suited to its environment.

GERMINATE: The process in which a seed begins to grow or sprout.

HERBIVORE: An animal or insect that eats plants.

INDIGENOUS PEOPLE: The original, native people of a place.

LATEX: A milky fluid produced by many plants—most notably the rubber tree.

MATERIAL: A thing that makes up something else—in other words the stuff that stuff is made of!

PHOTOSYNTHESIS: A biological process carried out by green plants, which use the power of sunlight to create solid materials, as well as oxygen, out of water and carbon dioxide.

PITH: A spongy white plant tissue that helps to store and transport nutrients around a plant.

POLLINATION: When pollen from the male part of a plant is transferred to the female part of a plant.

NATURAL RESIN: A sticky, often antiseptic, substance produced by some plants and trees.

SUPERSTITION: An irrational belief in supernatural influences which can lead to good or bad luck.

About Jonathan Drori

Jonathan Drori CBE is a Board member of both Cambridge and Oxford Botanic Gardens and Honorary Professor at Birmingham University's Institute of Forest Research. Previously, he was a Trustee of the Eden Project and the Royal Botanic Gardens, Kew, and for BBC TV, was responsible for many science documentaries. He is known for his TED talks on botany, which have been viewed millions of times. Jon is the author of the best-selling books *Around the World In 80 Trees* and *Around the World in 80 Plants,* revealing how the worlds of trees and plants are intricately entwined with our own history, culture, and folklore. This is his first book for children. See more at www.jondrori.co.uk

Acknowledgements

Many thanks to Richard Barley MBE, Executive Director of Gardens at The Royal Botanic Gardens, Kew, for checking each botanical story.

MAGIC CAT PUBLISHING

The illustrations were created digitally
Set in Fraunces, Cabin, and Just Saying
Library of Congress Control Number 2024945291
ISBN 978-1-917366-06-9

Text © 2025 Jonathan Drori
Illustrations © 2025 Raxenne Maniquiz and Jiatong Liu
Book design by Nicola Price
Edited by Rachel Williams

First Published in North America in 2025 by Magic Cat Publishing, an imprint of Lucky Cat Publishing Ltd, Unit 2 Empress Works, 24 Grove Passage, London E2 9FQ, UK

All rights reserved. No portion of this book may be reproduced, stored in a retrieval system, or transmitted in any form or by any means, mechanical, electronic, photocopying, recording, or otherwise, without written permission from the publisher.

Printed and bound in China
10 9 8 7 6 5 4 3 2 1

Distributed by ABRAMS
195 Broadway, New York, NY 10007, USA